Year of Fa

*All booklets are published thanks to the
generous support of the members of the
Catholic Truth Society*

CATHOLIC TRUTH SOCIETY

PUBLISHERS TO THE HOLY SEE

Index

Preface

A large fan club

On the 1ˢᵗ of May, 2011, Pope John Paul II was
beatified by his successor Pope Benedict XVI
in St. Peters Square in the presence of more
than 1.5 million faithful. What possessed these
people, including a surprising number of young
people, to stand in the heat in a crowd for hours,
some six years after his death? Almost none of
them had ever spoken personally to Pope John
Paul II. Their experience had been limited to a
view from afar, or to a quick handshake for the
happy few. Yet they had welcomed this man into
their hearts.

His secret? He never kept anything for himself. His listeners felt that he truly cared for them and wished true happiness for each of them. In everything he said and did, John Paul II was completely focused on Jesus, with whom he had a very personal relationship. "*Anyone who sees me, sees the Father*", Jesus said (Jn 14,9). In turn this blessed Pope showed Jesus to his flock. From the beginning of his pontificate he knew how to speak to the hearts of the faithful. "Open wide the doors to Christ", he said, raising his voice at the acceptance of his papacy. "Do not be afraid", he shouted to the crowd in St. Peter's Square. From the very beginning of his pontificate, JP2, as the young lovingly called him, had a special message for young people: "You are the future of the world and the hope of the Church! You are my hope!" (22 Oct. 1978).

Lolek

Karol Józef Wojtyła was born in Wadowice, Poland, on the 18th of May, 1920. From his earliest childhood Lolek, as his friends called him, loved sports. In 1938 he went to Kráków in order to study philology. He was also a talented writer, poet and actor. One year later the Nazis invaded Poland and he was forced into long years of arduous manual labour in a quarry. Together with others he founded a secret theatre. In this non-violent way, unlike that of some of his friends who took up arms, he took part in the resistance against the occupier. When in 1942 he discovered that God was calling him to the priesthood, he entered the clandestine seminary of Kraków.

Just after the Second World War, on the 1st of November 1946, Karol Wojtyła was ordained a priest. Shortly afterwards he was sent to Rome in order to continue his studies. He completed his doctorate in theology in 1948. During the summer months he visited a number of countries including France, Belgium and The Netherlands. In an article he wrote, he made an interesting comparison between these countries. He noticed how French Catholics had a particular interest in spiritual growth. The inhabitants of the Lower Countries on the other hand were occupied with practical and outward matters like the founding of unions. Would this be the reason that in the 1970s new ecclesial movements flourished in France, while the Dutch Church became divided by conflict?

'Uncle' Karol

After his studies, Wojtyła was appointed as a priest in various parishes and as a chaplain at the university. Father Wojtyła spent a lot of time with his students. He regularly organised walking, skiing and kayak trips through the mountains. On a simple altar made of stone or on an inverted kayak, they celebrated the Holy Eucharist daily. During these trips they spoke about every possible theme regarding the faith and daily life of young people. They could ask anything they wanted to their *wujek* (uncle) Karol and he would always give them a candid answer. Later his bishop asked him to continue his studies. He completed his doctorate in philosophy in 1953 and became professor of moral theology and social ethics. Both at the university and the seminary, he continued his conversation with young people.

In 1958 Wojtyla was appointed auxiliary bishop of Krákow. As a bishop he participated in the great ecclesiastical deliberations of the Second Vatican Council between 1962 and 1965. There he impressed the other bishops with his knowledge, his way of thinking and especially his engaging personality. He was appointed archbishop of Krákow in 1964 and he was elevated to the cardinalate three years later. Cardinal Wojtyła became a major opponent of communism. He continually pleaded for freedom, human rights and the position of the Church.

John Paul II

Twenty years after his episcopal ordination, Cardinal Wojtyła was elected Pope on the 16th of October 1978. He was the first non-Italian Pope after the Dutchman Adrian VI who died in 1523. The unknown Polish Pope made an unforget-

table impression on the crowds gathered at St. Peter's Square with his human and humble words: "If I make any mistakes in your, no in *our* language, please correct me." He demonstrated his great confidence in the intercession of Mary by inserting a large M in his papal coat of arms and by his motto: *Totus Tuus* (totally yours), Mary.

The first of his hundreds of trips brought John Paul II to Central America, where he showed the world a new way of being Pope. He achieved a great deal through his attention for truth and freedom for everyone. His visits to Poland and the diplomatic work of the Church contributed to the collapse of communism in Eastern Europe. His fierce but peaceful fight to obtain this did not make him loved by everyone: on the 13th of May 1981 he narrowly survived an attempt on his life.

Young people

Two years later the Pope invited young Catholics from all around the world to a meeting of prayer, sharing and joy in Rome in April 1984. The next year he proclaimed Palm Sunday to be the annual World Youth Day (20 DEC. 1985). No other Pope ever managed to engage so many people as John Paul II did. Over 5 million people gathered at World Youth Day in Manila in 1995. The enthusiastic crowd called out to him: "John Paul II, we love you!" The Pope responded: "I am an old man". And the crowd cried: "Lolek, Lolek!" At which the Pope responded with his particular sense of humour: "Lolek is not serious, John Paul II is too serious. You may call me Karol!"

His message was clear but not easy. Time and again he called on his listeners to dedicate themselves totally to Christ and to accept the consequences in their own lives. Still, the (young) people continued to come and listen to him. In his enthusiasm, he frequently

departed from his written text, much to the despair of his staff. He would then call himself back in line with a comment like: "Back to the text" (E.G. 13 JAN. 1995).

Amongst the subjects of his teaching are, for example, the importance of prayer, the Christian vocation, the defence of human life for everyone – also for the weakest – and the dignity of man, which is attacked by oppression, enslavement and consumerism. He proclaimed Jesus' message in terms of truth, peace, faith, freedom, liberation from fear, hope, and above all of love.

During the pontificate of Pope John Paul II, the moral influence of the Church increased. He wanted the Church to respond to the many modern challenges in the world. He started a worldwide New Evangelisation, using modern technology and communication methods. The Holy See gained diplomatic relationships with more and more countries. The Church's opinion on matters of peace, world population, human dignity and human rights, the position of minorities and human freedom, is now of great importance in world politics.

Charisma

Through his unique charisma, John Paul II deeply touched many people from all over the world. In him, they each recognised something of themselves. This Pope was both a poet and worker, actor and academic, a political activist and a world leader, a mystic and a priest. He looked at the world with an open and friendly eye, and let himself be touched by what happened around him. Many remember the tenderness with which he kissed a baby that was handed to him from the audience, but also the fierceness with which he called out during the Angelus: "No more war!" (16 MAR. 2003). Furthermore he was a simple man without pretentions. Notwithstanding his heavy responsibilities, he always remained himself. He

had attention for the people around him and had a love for Polish jokes and desserts.

The true source of the charisma of John Paul II can be found in his personal relationship with Christ. Everything he said and did was based on this indestructible foundation. The only way to understand this mystic Pope is by considering the way in which he devoted himself to God in everything. He rose early and started his day with prayer. He let prayer intentions from all over the world be brought up to his private chapel, so that he could pray for everyone. It is because of his intimate relationship with Jesus that he was able to speak everywhere with passion about the love for the Lord – in the streets, in churches or in stadiums all over the world.

A warm farewell

The Jubilee Year 2000 brought some 25 million pilgrims to Rome. The Pope repeated to the 2000 Dutch pilgrims what he had said earlier during World Youth Day, quoting Saint Catherine of Siena (Letter 368): "If you would be what you should be, you would set ablaze the entire earth" (7 nov. 2000). This was also a year of purification. The Pope asked forgiveness for the many wrongs done by people throughout the history of the Church.

During this year it was clearly visible that the Pope was ageing. Due to his illness it became more difficult for him to walk and speak. Nevertheless he continued his apostolate and thus became a living example of the dignity of man, one which is not affected by illness or age.

Pope John Paul II died on the 2nd of April, 2005, whilst thousands of faithful were gathered in St. Peter's Square, praying beneath his window. During several days the traffic around St Peter's was blocked by a queue of several kilometres, in which people were patiently waiting until it was their turn to personally take leave of this great Pope. In total some 4 million pilgrims came to Rome in order to show their affection and to pray for the deceased Pope.

This book does not have the pretension to give a complete overview or a full anthology of his life. It contains a selection of some short texts and pictures of his pontificate, which lasted over twenty-six years. The book is intended to help consider the message of blessed Pope John Paul II and discover its great value to today's world.

Father Michel Remery

Rotterdam Diocese and the
Faculty of Catholic Theology, Tilburg University

Faith and the Message
of Blessed John Paul II

What is 'faith'? Like a precious stone, the meaning of the word has many faces or aspects, each one of which conveys only a partial understanding. One aspect of faith (sometimes called the objective aspect) is about what a person believes, and in this sense 'faith' can be written down as a series of statements. The most important such series is the 'Creed' (from the Latin word Credo, meaning 'I believe'), which summarises the truths of the Catholic Christianity regarding God, the Church and the hope of eternal life. Contrary to some claims, especially by modern atheists, such statements of faith are not 'beliefs without evidence,' but have been tested and accepted on the basis of many kinds of testimony, coherence and fruitfulness for many centuries. Yet faith also has another aspect (sometimes called the subjective aspect) implying assent and trust. For example, the words of the Creed not only describe, but express personal trust in God and in the Church and in the hope of eternal life.

Yet even these aspects together do not completely reveal what is meant by 'faith', and it is to understand the deeper meaning that the life and words of Blessed John Paul II are so important for the Year of Faith. As shown repeatedly in this selection of his homilies, messages and addresses, faith is the beginning or root of a new kind of life. In this supernatural life of grace, a person does not simply know about God and trust in God, but knows God, loves God and seeks the face of God. So, for example, in his message to World Youth Day, 8 March 2003, the Pope exclaimed, 'Christianity is Christ! It is a Person, a Living Person!' an appeal that underlined his own personal relationship with Christ (as Father Remery remarks in his preface) and the urgency with which he poured out his entire life in inviting others to open wide their hearts to this joy.

Faith is therefore the root of a relationship with God that is personal (or, more precisely, 'second-personal'). Hence also the texts in this booklet emphasise how it is the quality of this relationship, and not any natural ability, that bears fruit for the Kingdom of Heaven. Blessed John Paul II witnessed to this truth himself by putting prayer and the sacraments first in his life, and by his special dedication and devotion to Mary, the Mother of Jesus.

Father Michel Remery and the Catholic Truth Society hope that these texts, drawn from a great diversity of writings and collated here in an accessible form, will serve to teach and inspire many throughout the Year of Faith and beyond. To conclude on a personal note, I would like to add that Father Remery, one of a new generation of young priests in Europe, was inspired to deepen his own Catholic faith through attending a World Youth Day and was later called to the priesthood. He is himself, therefore, one of the many and ongoing fruits of the ministry of Blessed Pope John Paul II, whose life, teachings and intercession will, I pray, also prove fruitful for you.

Father Andrew Pinsent

*Arundel and Brighton Diocese and the
Faculty of Theology, Oxford University*

Christ

"You are the Christ, the Son of the living God" (Mt
16:16). These words were spoken by Simon, son of
Jonah, in the district of Caesarea Philipi. Yes, he
spoke them with his own tongue, with a deeply
lived and experienced conviction, but it is not
in him that they find their source, their origin:
*"because it was not flesh hand blood that revealed
this to you but my Father in heaven"* (Mt 16:17).
They were the words of Faith. (...)

On this day and in this place these same
words must again be uttered and listened to:
"You are the Christ, the Son of the living God".
Yes, Brothers and sons and daughters, these
words first of all. Their content reveals to our
eyes the mystery of the living God, the mystery
to which the Son has brought us close. Nobody,
in fact, has brought the living God as close to
men and revealed him as he alone did. In our
knowledge of God, in our journey towards God,

we are totally linked to the power of these words: *"He who sees me sees the Father"* (Jn 14:9). (...) All of you who are still seeking God, all of you who already have the inestimable good fortune to believe, and also you who are tormented by doubt: please listen once again, today in this sacred place, to the words uttered by Simon Peter. In those words is the faith of the Church. In those same words is the new truth, indeed, the ultimate and definitive truth about man: the son of the living God. *"You are the Christ, the Son of the living God."* (...)

The new Successor of Peter in the See of Rome, today makes a fervent, humble and trusting prayer: 'Christ, make me become and remain the servant of your unique power, the servant of your sweet power, the servant of your power that knows no eventide. Make me be a servant. Indeed, the servant of your servants'.

Brothers and sisters, do not be afraid to welcome Christ and accept his power. Help the Pope and all those who wish to serve Christ and with Christ's power to serve the human person and the whole of mankind.

Do not be afraid. Open wide the doors to Christ. To his saving power open the boundaries of states, economic and political systems, the vast fields of culture, civilization and development. Do not be afraid. Christ knows 'what is in man'. He alone knows it. So often today man does not know what is within him, in the depths of his mind and heart. So often he is uncertain about the meaning of his life on this earth. He is assailed by doubt, a doubt which turns into despair.

We ask you therefore, we beg you with humility and trust, let Christ speak to man. He alone has words of life, yes, of eternal life.

Joannes Paulus PP II

22 October 1978, Mass at the beginning of the Pontificate at St Peter's Square

Jesus

The Pope wishes well to everyone, to each man and to all men, but he has a preference for the youngest, because they had a preferential place in the heart of Christ, who wished to remain with the children (Mᴋ 10:14; Lᴋ 18:16) and to talk to the young. He addressed his call to the young particularly (Mᴛ 19:21), and John, the youngest Apostle, was his favourite. (...) At this first meeting I wish to express to you, in addition to the intensity of my feelings of affection, my hope. Yes, my hope, because you are the promise of tomorrow. You are the hope of the Church and society.

Contemplating you, I think with trepidation and with trust of what is in store for you in life and of what you will be in the world of tomorrow, and I wish to leave you, as a compass for your lives, three thoughts: Look for Jesus, love Jesus, bear witness to Jesus. (...)

Look for Jesus, by reading and studying the Gospel, by reading some good books; look for Jesus by taking advantage in particular of the religious instruction lesson at school, of the catechisis, and of the meetings in your parishes. To look for Jesus personally, with the eagerness and joy of discovering the truth, gives deep inner satisfaction and great spiritual strength in order then to put into practice what he demands, even though it costs sacrifice. (...)

Love Jesus present in the Church by means of his priests; present in the family by means of your parents and those who love you. Love Jesus especially in those who are suffering in any way: physically, morally, spiritually. Let it be your commitment and programme to love your neighbour, discovering Christ's face in him.

Bear witness to Jesus with your courageous faith and your innocence. It is no use complaining of the wickedness of the times. As St Paul wrote, we must overcome evil by doing good (CFR. ROM 12:21). The world esteems and respects the courage of ideas and the strength of virtues. Do not be afraid to refuse words, acts, and attitudes which are not in conformity with Christian ideals. Be courageous in rejecting what destroys your innocence or wilts the freshness of your love for Christ.

To seek, love and bear witness to Jesus! This is your commitment; these are the instructions I leave you! By doing so, not only will you keep real joy in your lives, but also you will benefit the whole of society, which needs, above all, consistency with the evangelical message. This is what I wish you from the bottom of my heart.

Joannes Paulus PP. II

8 November 1978, Address to Italian youth in St Peter's

Consecrated life

"I came so that they might have life and have it more abundantly" (Jn 10:10). (...) With these words, the Lord Jesus reveals to us the mystery of the Christian vocation, and in particular the mystery of every vocation totally consecrated to God and the Church. This vocation consists in being called to offer one's life so that others may have life and have it abundantly. This is what was done by Jesus, the model of everyone who is called and consecrated: *"Behold, I come to do your will"* (Heb 10:9). And for this reason he gave his life, so that others might have life. This is what must be done by every man or woman who is called to follow Christ is total self-giving.

A vocation is a call to life: to receive it and to give it. (...) Just as the Lord Jesus came to give life, so he instituted the Church, his Body, so that in it believers might share his life (cfr. Lumen Gentium 7). (...) How could we reasonably pray for vocations unless our prayer were effectively accompanied by a sincere question about conversion?

Those living consecrated lives, I invite earnestly and with particular affection to examine their own lives. Their vocation, totally consecrated to God and the Church, must be lived to a rhythm of 'receiving and giving'. They have received much; they must give much. (...) Their witness and cooperation correspond to the loving dispositions of God's providence (cfr.r.. OT 2).

With sincere confidence I invite all believing families to reflect upon the mission they have received from God for the education of their children in the faith and in Christian living. It is a mission that also involves their children's vocations "The education of children should be such that when they grow up they will be able to follow their vocation, including a religious vocation, and choose their state of life with full consciousness of responsibility" (GAUDIUM ET SPES 52). Cooperation between families and the Church for vocations has deep roots in the mystery and the 'ministry' of the Christian family, (...) "the primary and most excellent seedbed of vocations to a life of consecration to the Kingdom of God" (FAMILIARIS CONSORTIO, 53). (...)

Lord Jesus, grant the abundance of your life to all those who are consecrated to you for the service of the Church. Make them happy in their self-giving, indefatigable in their ministry, generous in their sacrifice. May their example open new hearts to listening and following your call. (...)

Lord Jesus, grant the abundance of your life to all those whom you are calling to your service, especially young men and women; enlighten them in making their choices; help them in their difficulties; support them in their faithfulness; make them enthusiastic and courageous in offering their lives, in accordance with your example, so that others may have life.

Joannes Paulus II

2 February 1982, Message for the XIX World Day for Vocations

Priests

The foundation and at the same time the secret of your priestly identity is in the awareness of being called by God (...) Called, consecrated, sent. This threefold dimension explains and determines your behaviour and your way of life. You are 'set apart', 'segregated' but not 'separated' (CFR. PRESBYTERORUM ORDINIS, 3). In this way you can dedicate yourself to the work you are about being entrusted with: serving your brothers. You then understand that the consecration you are receiving entirely devotes you, makes out of you living instruments of the adoption of Christ in the world, of the prolongation of his mission for the glory for the Father.

The complete donation of yourselves to the Lord aims at this. That complete donation which is striving for sanctity. It is the inner task to 'imitate what you handle'. (...) It is grace and personal commitment to imitate Christ, to reproduce in your ministry and in your behaviour this image engraved by the fire of the Spirit. The image of Christ, priest and victim, of the crucified redeemer.

In this framework of complete donation, of union with Christ and of communion with his exclusive and final dedication to the work of the Father, one understands the obligation of celibacy. It is the expression of a full donation, of a particular consecration, of an absolute willingness.

The response to the gift that God grants in priesthood is the donation of the elected one with his entire being, with his heart and his body, with the spousal meaning that clerical celibacy has with reference to the love of Christ and to the complete donation to the community of the Church.

The soul of this donation is love. In order to live celibacy one does not give up love, the power to live love and to be a sign of love in life. The heart and all powers of a priest are impregnated with the love of Christ, with the aim of being witness of a boundless pastoral charity right in the middle of the brothers. (...)

Don't be afraid that in this way you may end up separated from your faithful and from the ones to whom you are assigned by your mission. You would be separated from them much more radically if you forgot or neglected the meaning of the consecration that marks your priesthood. To be 'yet another one', at work, in your lifestyle, in the way you dress, in political involvement, would not help you in fulfilling your mission. On the contrary, you would defraud your faithful who wish you to be entirely priests, like Christ, brothers and friends.

Joannes Paulus PP. II

8 November 1982, Homily during the priestly Ordinations in Valencia, Spain

Mary

Blest are you, Mary who believed. Thus we praise you along with Elizabeth (CFR. LK 1:45). Blest are you, Mother of our Lord Jesus and of the Church. (...)

To your motherly heart, Mary we especially entrust those who are oppressed by suffering and sorrow: the sick and handicapped, men and women experiencing difficult marriages, the children of families in conflict, men with large debts, the unemployed, the alienated and imprisoned. How many tears, how much fear, how much darkness on this journey!

May the Cross of your Son shine before them as the symbol of God's Infinite mercy. Reveal to them Christ's spirit, which enables them to conquer evil with good (CFR. ROM 12:21), to give new meaning to life with courageous love. Merciful Mary, accept every unselfish act of a good Samaritan, every hour offered voluntarily in service of a suffering neighbour!

In the same way we commend to you men in the full bloom of life, men and women with family responsibilities, committed to the community of the nation. Let them find in the Good News light and strength for their own ideas and decisions, guided by a mature Christian conscience: fathers and mothers, teachers and doctors, scientists and politicians, police, soldiers and all those who work for the good of the community. Reveal to them the shining value of truth, the great good of justice, the silent splendour of altruism!

We invoke your motherly protection, O Mary, also for the younger generations: infants, boys and girls, young men and women. Lead them gently, step by step, along the path of Christian responsibility to themselves and to the community: the courageous and the strong, the enterprising and active, as well as those who are silent, who hesitate, who are indecisive, those who laugh often and those who are always serious.

Do not let the light go out in their hearts, the light of those ideals which give the life of man its true meaning. May no one neglect them: neither young people themselves, nor anyone else. Mother, bless the youth that they may be able to demand much of themselves and give much to others, to resist the temptations of a world of pleasures and to promise to promote the good of their neighbour. (...)

Mother of the Church, reveal again to the People of God of this nation the way to discover and promote new vocations to the priesthood and to religious life. (...) Christ, Good Shepherd of your flock, welcome in your Mother's heart all our faith, our good will and our sincere dedication.

Amen.

Joannes Paulus II

13 September 1983, Prayer to Mary in Mariazell, Austria

Suffering

All of you, both with your suffering and with your loving assistance to the suffering ones, are called to be apostles and witnesses of Christ. Here in your country, I am thinking of your great predecessors in the faith: (...) and particularly of Ludwina of Schiedam. You know how at the age of fifteen, after a fall on ice, she suffered the martyrdom of being confined to bed for thirty-eight years. At the beginning she was certainly no more pious that her peers: she was impatient by nature. For many years she was bombarded within herself by the question, 'Why me?' Rebellion and discouragement followed, right up to the moment when, guided by the Spirit of God, she began with the passing of years to understand this secret: her sufferings could become the journey of love. (...)

A person who must endure suffering can know he has a bond, in faith, with God, who always has pity for the person who suffers.

Christ did not give a direct answer to the understandable question. 'Why is there so much suffering in our world?' However, with his suffering, with his Death and Resurrection, he transformed human suffering from within and, we could say, filled it with his presence.

Jesus identifies himself so much with man, especially with suffering man and with those who try to alleviate suffering and endure it, that one day he will say 'I was ill, I was thirsty, I was a stranger, I was in prison,' (Mt 25:35-36), I saw no way out, I was alone, I was afraid.

And with all that, the responsibility lies with all of us to be on guard not to cause each other suffering and to free our neighbour from pain. Most especially we who know we have been called to follow in the footsteps of the Lord, who, wherever he was, did nothing but good. We too recite in prayer what the Lord himself taught us: "Deliver us from evil".

Yes, deliver us from evil, the source of human sufferings, deliver us from our selfishness, which makes so many people suffer, deliver us likewise from unexpected suffering. Deliver us from suffering in all its forms: natural catastrophes, hunger, illness, loneliness, war, persecutions, discrimination and suspicion.

Deliver us from the evil by which men do not share in the goods of the earth, in which they have a right to share.

It is especially in you, brothers and sisters in Jesus Christ, that the Church sees the source and the artisans par excellence of the divine strength that lies in her. Indeed, looking at you, who are sharing Christ's sufferings, the Church can realize that you are capable of keeping hope alive, the hope that gives meaning to suffering endured out of love; that you, as Christians, full of joy, can by the witness of your faith walk in the footsteps of the Virgin Mary. (...)

Open the doors of your hearts to the Lord, since you too must be witnesses of his presence and his consolation!

Joannes Paulus II

13 May 1985, Homily to the sick and disabled in The Hague, The Netherlands

Human Rights

In general, we much promote a certain conception of man which is founded upon an authentic humanism. We must not allow the human person to suffer from actions which diminish him, becoming in some way an object in a materialist vision which sees only his economic value, or which is willing to sacrifice him as a means to manipulate him in various ways. The same thing holds true regarding the dignity of every race.

The fundamental principle will always be the dignity of the human person, respect for his inalienable fundamental rights, which are invoked by the majority of our contemporaries but which in reality are trampled upon in certain regions of the earth.

Among these rights is naturally found respect for human life in all phases of its development, from conception to old age, and also respect for the human embryo, which cannot be subjected to experiments as though it were an object.

41

These rights also regard the dignity of our lives, that is the material possibilities for living decently, but also freedom of mind, of opinions, of convictions and of beliefs, in so far as these beliefs themselves respect the other. This implies the banning of torture, of internment, and of the other degrading practices designed to punish crimes of opinion. Dignity demands in particular that no obstacles be placed before conscience, religion and religious practice, or before the means necessary for the formation of the faith and participation in worship, in stable communities

Dignity is also the refusal of every compromise with terrorism – which uses the lives and goods of innocent persons as means – and this no matter what the motives invoked by it. (...)

Dignity is the seeking of a just solution for the refugees who have had to leave their own countries because of war or political intolerance and who live in great numbers in camps, isolated and often in a state of intolerable neglect. Finally, dignity is clearly respect for the cultures of diverse human groups, and the elimination of all racial discrimination (...)

But it is not solely a question of rejecting violence or that which offends against fundamental rights in a flagrant way. It is a question of undertaking positive actions that express our solidarity in order to help men to respond to their profound needs.

Joannes Paulus M̄

20 May 1985, Address to the Civil Authorities and the Diplomatic Corps in the Royal Castle of Laken, Belgium

Joy

I have said before on another occasion: "In a true sense, joy is the keynote of the Christian message" (2 OCT. 1979). As I said then, my wish is that the Christian message may bring joy to all who open their hearts to it: "joy to children, joy to parents, joy to families and to friends, joy to workers and scholars, joy to the sick and to the elderly, joy to all humanity". (...)

Faith is our source of joy. We believe in a God who created us so that we might enjoy human happiness - in some measure on earth, in its fullness in heaven.

We are meant to have our human joys: the joy of living, the joy of love and friendship, the joy of work well done.

We who are Christians have a further cause for joy: like Jesus, we know that we are loved by God our Father. This love transforms our lives and fills us with joy. It makes us see that Jesus did not come to lay burdens upon us. He came to teach us what it means to be fully happy and fully human. Therefore, we discover joy when we discover truth - the truth about God our Father, the truth about Jesus our Saviour, the truth about the Holy Spirit who lives in our hearts.

We do not pretend that life is all beauty. We are aware of darkness and sin, of poverty and pain. But we know Jesus has conquered sin and passed through his own pain to the glory of the Resurrection. And we live in the light of his Paschal Mystery - the mystery of his Death and Resurrection. 'We are an Easter People and Alleluia is our song!'.

We are not looking for a shallow joy but rather a joy that comes from faith, that grows through unselfish love, that respects the 'fundamental duty of love of neighbour, without which it would be unbecoming to speak of Joy'. We realize that joy is demanding; it demands unselfishness; it demands a readiness to say with Mary: *"Be it done unto me according to thy word".* (Lk 1:38).

Mary, our Mother: I turn to you and with the Church I invoke you as Mother of holy Joy (*Mater plena sanctae laetitiae*). (...) Help all your children to see that the good things in their lives come to them from God the Father through your Son Jesus Christ. Help them to experience in the Holy Spirit the joy which filled your own Immaculate Heart. And in the midst of the sufferings and trials of life may they find the fullness of joy that belongs to the victory of your Crucified Son, and comes forth from his Sacred Heart.

Joannes Paulus II

30 November 1986, Angelus in Adelaide, Australia

Vocation

Dear young Friends, I think you already know, without my saying it, how happy I am to be with you today. (...) From my early days as a young priest, I have spent many hours talking with students on university campuses or while hiking along lakes or in the mountains and hills. (...)

As you probably know, I often say that you who are young bring hope to the world. The future of the world shines in your eyes. Even now, you are helping to shape the future of society. Since I have always placed high hopes in young people, I would like to speak to you today precisely about hope.

We cannot live without hope. We have to have some purpose in life, some meaning to our existence. We have to aspire to something. Without hope, we begin to die. (...) Hope comes from God, from our belief in God. People of hope are those who believe God created them for a purpose and that he will provide for their needs. They believe that God loves them as a faithful Father. (...)

Dear young friends: I pray that your faith in Christ will always be lively and strong. In this way, you will 'always be ready to tell others the reason for your hope' (1Pt 3,15) you will be messengers of hope for the world.

I am often asked, especially by young people, why I became a priest. May be some of you would like to ask the same question. Let me try briefly to reply.

I must begin by saying that it is impossible to explain entirely, for it remains a mystery, even to myself. How does one explain the ways of God? Yet, I know that at a certain point in my life, I became convinced that Christ was saying to me what he had said to thousands before me: 'Come, follow me!' There was a clear sense that what I heard in my heart was no human voice, nor was it just an idea of my own. Christ was calling me to serve him as a priest.

And you can probably tell, I am deeply grateful to God for my vocation to the priesthood. Nothing means more to me or gives me greater joy than to celebrate Mass each day and to serve God's people in the Church. That has been true ever since the day of my ordination as a priest. Nothing has ever changed it, not even becoming Pope.

Confiding this to you, I would like to invite each of you to listen carefully to God's voice in your heart. Every human person is called to communion with God. That is why the Lord made us, to know him and love him and serve him, and - in doing this - to find the secret to lasting joy.

Joannes Paulus II

15 September 1987, Teleconference with the young people in the Universal Amphitheatre, Los Angeles, United States

Marriage

You have come to this Monte del Gozo (Mount of Joy), full of hopeful anticipation and confidence, setting aside the snares of the world, truly to meet Jesus, "the Way, the Truth and the Life" (Jn 14:6), who has invited each one of you to follow him lovingly. (...) Christ asks you personally if you want to follow decidedly the way which he is showing you, if you are prepared to accept his truth, his message of salvation, if you want to live the Christian ideal fully. (...)

But, more than one of you is asking himself or herself: What does Jesus want of me? To what is he calling me? What is the meaning of his call for me? For the great majority of you, human love will present itself as a way of self-realization in the formation of a family. This is why, in the name of Christ I want to ask you: Are you prepared to follow the call of Christ through the Sacrament of Marriage, so as to be procreators of new life? (...)

The family is a mystery of love, because it collaborates directly in the creative work of God. Beloved young people, a large sector of society does not accept Christ's teachings, and, consequently, it takes other roads: hedonism, divorce, abortion, birth control and contraceptive methods. These ways of understanding life are in clear contrast to the Law of God and the teachings of the Church. To follow Christ faithfully means putting the Gospel message into practice, and this also implies chastity, the defence of life, and also the indissolubility of the matrimonial bond, which is not a mere contract which can be arbitrarily broken.

Living in the 'permissiveness' of the modern world, which denies or minimizes the authenticity of Christian principles, it is easy and attractive to breathe in this contaminated mentality and give in to the passing desire. But, bear in mind that those who act in this way neither follow Christ nor love him. To love means to walk together in the same direction towards God, who is the Source of Love. In this Christian framework, love is stronger than death. (...) Therefore I ask you again: Are you prepared to protect human life with the maximum care at every moment, even in the most difficult? Are you prepared, as young Christians, to live and defend love through indissoluble marriage, to protect the stability of the family, a stability which favours the balanced upbringing of children, under the protection of a paternal and maternal love, which complement each other?

This is the Christian witness that is expected of the majority of you, young men and women. To be a Christian means to be a witness to Christian truth, and today, particularly, it is to put into practice the authentic meaning which Christ and the Church give to life and to the full realization of young men and women through marriage and the family.

Joannes Paulus II

19 August 1989, Address on mount Gozo,
Santiago de Compostella, Spain

Evangelization

"God so loved the world that he gave his only Son" (JN 3:16). Jesus, sent by the Father to mankind, communicates the abundance of life to every believer (CFR. JN 10:10). (...) His Gospel must become 'communication' and mission. The missionary vocation summons every Christian; it becomes the very essence of every testimony of concrete and living faith.

It is a mission which traces its origins from the Father's plan, the plan of love and salvation which is carried out through the power of the Spirit, without which every apostolic initiative is destined to failure.

It is to enable his disciples to carry out this mission that Jesus says to them: *"Receive the Holy Spirit"* (JN 20:22). He thus transmits to the Church his own saving mission, so that the Easter mystery may continue to be communicated to every person, in every age, in every corner of the globe.

You, young people, are especially called to become missionaries of this New Evangelization, by daily witnessing to the Word that saves. You personally experience the anxieties of the present historical period, fraught with hope and doubt, in which it can at times be easy to lose the way that leads to the encounter with Christ.

In fact, numerous are the temptations of our time, the seductions that seek to muffle the divine voice resounding within the heart of each individual. To the people of our century, to all of you, dear young people, who hunger and thirst for truth, the Church offers herself as a travelling companion. She offers the eternal Gospel message and entrusts you with an exalting apostolic task: to be the protagonists of the New Evangelization. As the faithful guardian and representative of the wealth of faith transmitted to her by Christ, she is ready to enter into dialogue with the new generations; in order to answer their needs and expectations and to find in frank and open dialogue the most appropriate way to reach the source of divine salvation.

The Church entrusts to young people the task of proclaiming to the world the joy which springs from having met Christ. Dear friends, allow yourselves to be drawn to Christ; accept his invitation and follow him. Go and preach the Good News that redeems (CFR. MT 28:19) .

To you young people the task of becoming communicators of hope and peacemakers is entrusted in a special way (CFR. MT 5:9) in a world that is ever more in need of credible witnesses and consistent messengers. Know how to speak to the hearts of your contemporaries, who thirst for truth and happiness, in a constant, even if often unconscious, search for God.

Joannes Paulus II

21 November 1993, Message for the IX en X World Youth Day

Mission

"As the Father has sent me, so am I sending you" (JN 20:21). Two thousand years ago these words set in motion the Church's never-ending mission to proclaim the Gospel of salvation to the ends of the earth.

The Lord Jesus said to the Apostles: *"Receive the Holy Spirit"* (JN 20:21), and the mission – in obedience to these words – began on the day of Pentecost, when the Holy Spirit came upon the Apostles and those simple men became the holders of the divine power which enabled them to announce the Gospel with courage, even to the shedding of their blood.

What do these words mean today? (...) It is always Christ who sends. But whom does he send? You, young people, are the ones he looks upon with love. Christ, who says: 'Follow me', wants you to live your lives with a sense of vocation. He wants your lives to have a precise meaning, a dignity. Most of you are called to marriage and family life; but some will receive a call to the priesthood or religious life. (...)

The World Youth Day can be for all of you an occasion for discovering your calling, for discerning the particular path which Christ sets before you. The search and discovery of God's will for you is a deep and fascinating endeavour. It requires of you the attitude of trust expressed in the words of the Psalm used in today's liturgy: *"You will show me the path to life, fullness of joy in your presence, the delights at your right hand forever"* (Ps 15(16):11).

Every vocation, every path to which Christ calls us, ultimately leads to fulfilment and happiness, because it leads to God, to sharing in God's own life. And I see that the people of the Philippines are very joyous. Why are they so joyous? I am convinced that you Filipino peoples are so joyous because you received the Good News. Who receives the Good News is joyous, is radiant with joy, and also gives the joy to others. Today they are giving that joy to the Pope. (...)

Returning to the text, do not be slow to answer the Lord's call! (...) I pray every day that the Catholic young people of the world will hear the call of Christ and that their response will be what the Responsorial Psalm says: *"The Lord is my allotted portion... I set the Lord ever before me; with him at my right hand I shall not be disturbed"* (Ps 15(16):8). (...) Enormous tasks lie before the youth of the world (...) and the Church constantly prays the Lord of the harvest to send them, to send us, to send you.

Joannes Paulus II

13 January 1995, Homily to the 'International Youth Forum' at the University of St Thomas, Manila, Philippines

Saints

You will ask me: but is it possible today to be saints? If we had to rely only on human strength, the undertaking would be truly impossible. You are well aware, in fact, of your successes and your failures; you are aware of the heavy burdens weighing on man, the many dangers which threaten him and the consequences caused by his sins. At times we may be gripped by discouragement and even come to think that it is impossible to change anything either in the world or in ourselves.

Although the journey is difficult, we can do everything in the One who is our Redeemer. Turn then to no one, except Jesus. Do not look elsewhere for that which only He can give you, because *"of all the names in the world given to men this is the only one by which we can be saved"*(Ac 4:12). With Christ, saintliness - the divine plan for every baptized person - becomes possible. Rely on Him; believe in the invincible power of the Gospel and place faith as the foundation of your hope. Jesus walks with you, he renews your heart and strengthens you with the vigour of his Spirit.

Young people of every continent, do not be afraid to be the saints of the new millennium! Be contemplative, love prayer; be coherent with your faith and generous in the service of your brothers and sisters, be active members of the Church and builders of peace. To succeed in this demanding project of life, continue to listen to His Word, draw strength from the Sacraments, especially the Eucharist and Penance.

The Lord wants you to be intrepid apostles of his Gospel and builders of a new humanity. In fact, how could you say you believe in God made man without taking a firm position against all that destroys the human person and the family? If you believe that Christ has revealed the Father's love for every person, you cannot fail to strive to contribute to the building of a new world, founded on the power of love and forgiveness, on the struggle against injustice and all physical, moral and spiritual distress, on the orientation of politics, economy, culture and technology to the service of man and his integral development. (...)

The mystery of the Incarnation of the Son of God and that of the Redemption he worked for all men, constitute the central message of our faith. The Church proclaims this down through the centuries, walking "amidst the misunderstandings and persecutions of the world and the consolations of God" (St Augustine, De Civitate Dei 18,51,2). and she entrusts it to her children as a precious treasure to be safeguarded and shared. (...) Meanwhile, gladly and with great affection, I bless all of you, with your families and your loved ones.

Joannes Paulus II

29 July 1999, Message for the XV World Youth Day

Peace

Jesus' first words to the disciples after the Resurrection were: *"Peace be with you"* (Jn 20:19, 21:26). Christ came to unite what was divided, to destroy sin and hatred, and to reawaken in humanity the vocation to unity and brotherhood. (...)

The Church vividly remembers her Lord and intends to confirm her vocation and mission to be in Christ a 'Sacrament' or sign and instrument of peace in the world and for the world. For the Church, to carry out her evangelizing mission means to work for peace. (...)

It is a sign of hope that, despite many serious obstacles, initiatives for peace continue to spring up day by day, with the generous cooperation of many people. Peace is a building constantly under construction.

The building up of peace involves:

- parents who are examples and witnesses of peace in their families, and who educate their children for peace;

- teachers who are able to pass on the genuine values present in every field of knowledge and in the historical and cultural heritage of humanity;

- working men and women, who are committed to extending their age-old struggle for the dignity of work to those present-day situations which, at the international level, cry out for justice and solidarity;

- political leaders who put at the heart of their own political activity and of that of their countries a firm and unwavering determination to promote peace and justice;

- those in International Organizations who, often with scarce resources, work in the front line where being "peace-makers" can involve risking their own personal safety; (...)

- believers who, convinced that authentic faith is never a source of war or violence, spread convictions of peace and love through ecumenical and interreligious dialogue.

I am thinking particularly of you, dear young people, who experience in a special way the blessing of life and have a duty not to waste it. In your schools and universities, in the work-place, in leisure and sports, in all that you do, let yourselves be guided by this constant thought: peace within you and peace around you, peace always, peace with everyone, peace for everyone. (...)

Make every effort to rediscover the path of reconciliation and forgiveness. It is a difficult path, but it is the only one which will enable you to look to the future with hope for yourselves, your children, your countries and all humanity.

Joannes Paulus PP. II

8 December 1999, Message for the XXXIII World Day for Peace

I believe

Dear young friends, today I wish to tell you that I believe firmly in Jesus Christ our Lord. Yes, I believe. (...) I remember how as a child, in my own family, I learned to pray and trust in God. I remember the life in the parish that I attended in Wadowice, as well as the parish of Saint Stanislaus Kostka, in Debniki in Kraków, where I received my basic formation in Christian living.

I cannot forget the experience of the war and the years of work in a factory. My priestly vocation came to its full maturity during the Second World War, during the occupation of Poland. The tragedy of the War gave a particular colouring to the gradual maturing of my vocation in life. In these circumstances, I perceived a light shining ever more brightly within me: the Lord wanted me to be a priest! I remember with feeling that moment in my life when, on the morning of 1 November 1946, I was ordained a priest.

My Credo continues in my present service to the Church. On 16 October 1978, after my election to the See of Peter, when I was asked 'Do you accept?', I answered 'With obedience in faith to Christ, my Lord, and trusting in the Mother of Christ and of the Church, no matter what the difficulties, I accept' (RED. HOM., 2). From that time on, I have tried to carry out my mission, drawing light and strength every day from the faith that binds me to Christ.

But my faith, like that of Peter and like the faith of each one of you, is not just my doing, my attachment to the truth of Christ and the Church. It is essentially and primarily the work of the Holy Spirit, a gift of his grace. The Lord gives his Spirit to me as he gives Him to you, to help us say: 'I believe', and then to use us to bear witness to him in every corner of the world. (...)

Dear friends, why do I want to offer you this personal testimony? (...) I do so in order to make it clear that the journey of faith is part of everything that happens in our lives. God is at work in the concrete and personal situations of each one of us. (...)

Do not let the time that the Lord gives you go by as though everything happened by chance. Saint John has told us that everything has been made in Christ. Therefore, believe unshakeably in him. He directs the history of individuals as well as the history of humanity. Certainly Christ respects our freedom, but in all the joyful or bitter circumstances of life he never stops asking us to believe in him, in his word, in the reality of the Church, in eternal life!

Joannes Paulus II

15 August 2000, Address for the XV World Youth Day at St Peter's Square

Follow me

Dear young people, do not doubt God's love for you! He has reserved for you a place in his heart and a mission in the world. The first reaction can be fear or doubt. These are sentiments which Jeremiah felt before you: *"Ah, Lord God! Behold, I do not know how to speak, for I am only a youth"* (Jr 1:6). The task seems immense, because it assumes the dimensions of society and the world. But do not forget that when the Lord calls, he also provides the necessary strength and grace to answer his call.

Do not be afraid to accept your responsibilities: the Church needs you, she needs your commitment and generosity; the Pope needs you and, at the beginning of this new millennium, he is asking you to take the Gospel on the paths of the world. (...)

The Risen One asks Peter the question that will determine his whole life: *"Simon, son of John, do you love me?"* (Jn 21:16). Jesus does not ask him what his talents, gifts and skills are. Nor does he ask the one who had just denied him whether from now on he will be faithful to him, whether he will stand firm. He asks him the only thing that matters, the one thing that can give a vocation its foundation: *"Do you love me?"*

Today Christ is asking each of you the same question: do you love me? He is not asking you whether you know how to speak to crowds, whether you can direct an organization or manage an estate. He is asking you to love him. All the rest will ensue. In fact, walking in Jesus' footsteps is not immediately expressed in things to do or say, but first of all in loving him, in staying with him, in totally accepting him into one's life.

Today you are giving Jesus' question a sincere answer. Some will be able to say with Peter: *"Lord; you know that I love you!"* (Jn 21:16). Others will say: 'Lord, you know how I would like to love you; teach me to love you, to be able to follow you'. The important thing is to stay on the path, to continue the journey without losing sight of the goal, until the day when you will be able to say with all your heart: *"You know that I love you!"*.

Dear young people, love Christ and love the Church! Love Christ as he loves you. Love the Church as Christ loves her. Do not forget that true love sets no conditions; it does not calculate or complain but simply loves. How could you in fact be responsible for an inheritance which you only partly accepted? How can one share in building something that one does not love with all one's heart? May communion in the Body and Blood of the Lord help everyone grow in love for Jesus and for his Body, which is the Church.

Joannes Paulus II

17 August 2000, Homily to the 'International Youth Forum' in Castel Gandolfo

Eucharist

The Eucharist is the sacrament of the presence of Christ, who gives himself to us because he loves us. He loves each one of us in a unique and personal way in our practical daily lives: in our families, among our friends, at study and work, in rest and relaxation. He loves us when he fills our days with freshness, and also when, in times of suffering, he allows trials to weigh upon us: even in the most severe trials, he lets us hear his voice.

Yes, dear friends, Christ loves us and he loves us for ever! He loves us even when we disappoint him, when we fail to meet his expectations for us. He never fails to embrace us in his mercy. How can we not be grateful to this God who has redeemed us, going so far as to accept the foolishness of the Cross? To God who has come to be at our side and has stayed with us to the end?

To celebrate the Eucharist, 'to eat his flesh and drink his blood', means to accept the wisdom of the Cross and the path of service. It means that we signal our willingness to sacrifice ourselves for others, as Christ has done.

Our society desperately needs this sign, and young people need it even more so, tempted as they often are by the illusion of an easy and comfortable life, by drugs and pleasure-seeking, only to find themselves in a spiral of despair, meaninglessness and violence.

It is urgent to change direction and to turn to Christ. This is the way of justice, solidarity and commitment to building a society and a future worthy of the human person. This is our Eucharist, this is the answer that Christ wants from us, from you young people. (...) Jesus is no lover of half measures, and he does not hesitate to pursue us with the question: *"Will you also go away?"* (Jn 6:67). In the presence of Christ, the Bread of Life, we too want to say today with Peter: *"Lord, to whom shall we go? You have the words of eternal life!"* (Jn 6:68). (...)

I entrust to you, dear friends, this greatest of God's gifts to us. (...) I ask the Lord therefore to raise up from among you many holy vocations to the priesthood. Today as always the Church needs those who celebrate the Eucharistic Sacrifice with a pure heart. The world must not be deprived of the gentle and liberating presence of Christ living in the Eucharist! (...) In a special way, may sharing in the Eucharist lead to a new flourishing of vocations to the religious life. In this way the Church will have fresh and generous energies for the great task of the new evangelization.

Joannes Paulus II

20 August 2000, Homily during the closing celebration of the XV World Youth Day at Tor Vergata, Rome

God speaks

"Lord, to whom shall we go? You have the words of eternal life!" (Jn 6:68). (...) The Apostle Peter spoke these words to Jesus, who had presented himself to the crowds as the bread come down from heaven to give life to men (cfr. Jn 6:58). Today I have the joy of repeating these words in your presence, indeed of repeating them in your name and together with you.

Today Christ asks you the same question that he asked the Apostles: *"Will you also go away?"*. (Jn 6:67). (...) And you, how do you reply? I am sure that with me you too will make your own the words of Peter: *"Lord, to whom shall we go? You have the words of eternal life"*. (...)

Yes, dear young people, Christ has the *"words of eternal life"*. His words last for ever and above all they open for us the gates of eternal life. When God speaks, his words give life, they call things into existence, they direct our journey, they restore disappointed and broken hearts and pour fresh hope into them.

Reading the Bible, we discover right from the first page that God speaks to us. He speaks to us as he gives life to creation: the heavens, the earth, light, water, living things, man and woman, everything exists by his word. His word gives meaning to all things, rescuing them from chaos. For this reason nature is an immense book in which we can see with ever fresh wonder the traces of divine Beauty.

Even more than in creation, God speaks in the story of humanity. He reveals his presence in world events, by beginning time after time a dialogue with men and women created in his image, in order to establish with each one of them a communion of life and love. History becomes a journey in which the Creator and the individual come to know each other, a dialogue of which the ultimate purpose is to lead us our of the slavery of sin to the freedom of love.

Dear young people, when lived in this way, history becomes a path to freedom. Do you wish to travel this path? Do you too wish to be part of this adventure? (...) The future of the world and of the Church depends also on your reply. (...)

Before leaving you, I wish to add a final word: love the Church! She is your family and the spiritual building of which you are called to be the living stones. (...)

And if the path will sometimes be steep, if the path of faithfulness to the Gospel will appear too demanding, because it will certainly require sacrifice and courageous decisions, remember our meeting. In this way you will be able to relive the enthusiasm of the profession of faith: (...) *"Lord, to whom shall we go? You have the words of eternal life."* Repeat it and do not fear! Christ will be your strength and your joy.

Joannes Paulus II

26 June 2001, Address to the Ukrainian youth in Lviv

Totus Tuus

Dear young people, in difficult times, which everyone experiences, you are not alone: like John at the foot of the Cross, Jesus also gives his Mother to you so that she will comfort you with her tenderness. (...) My dear young people, you are more or less the same age as John and you have the same desire to be with Jesus.

Today, it is you whom Jesus expressly asks to receive Mary 'into your home' and to welcome her 'as one of yours'; to learn from her the one who *"kept all these things, pondering them in her heart"* (Lk 2:19), that inner disposition to listen and the attitude of humility and generosity that singled her out as God's first collaborator in the work of salvation. She will discharge her ministry as a mother and train you and mould you until Christ is fully formed in you (CFR.. ROS. VIRG. MARIAE, 15).

This is why I now wish to repeat the motto of my episcopal and pontifical service:

Totus Tuus (all yours). Throughout my life I have experienced the loving and forceful presence of the Mother of Our Lord. Mary accompanies me every day in the fulfilment of my mission as Successor of Peter. Mary is Mother of divine grace, because she is the Mother of the Author of grace. Entrust yourselves to her with complete confidence! You will be radiant with the beauty of Christ.

Open up to the breath of the Spirit, and you will become courageous apostles, capable of spreading the fire of charity and the light of truth all around you. In Mary's school, you will discover the specific commitment that Christ expects of you, and you will learn to put Christ first in your lives, and to direct your thoughts and actions to him.

Dear young people, you know that Christianity is not an opinion nor does it consist of empty words. Christianity is Christ! It is a Person, a Living Person! To meet Jesus, to love him and make him loved: this is the Christian vocation.

Mary was given to you to help you enter into a more authentic and more personal relationship with Jesus. Through her example, Mary teaches you to gaze on him with love, for He has loved us first. Through her intercession, she forms in you a disciple's heart able to listen to her Son, who reveals the face of his Father and the true dignity of the human person. (...)

With Mary, the handmaiden of the Lord, you will discover the joy and fruitfulness of the hidden life. With her, disciple of the Master, you will follow Jesus along the streets of Palestine, becoming witnesses of his preaching and his miracles. With her, the sorrowful Mother, you will accompany Jesus in his passion and death. With her, Virgin of hope, you will welcome the festive Easter proclamation and the priceless gift of the Holy Spirit.

Joannes Paulus II

8 March 2003, Message for the XVIII World Youth Day

Cross

Twenty years ago at the end of the Holy Year of the Redemption, I entrusted to young people the Cross, the tree on which Christ was raised from the earth and lived that 'hour' for which he had come into the world! Since then this Cross, on pilgrimage from one Youth Day to the next, has been travelling across the world carried by young people. It proclaims the merciful love of God who meets the needs of all his creatures, to restore to them the dignity they have lost through sin. Thanks to you, dear friends, millions of young people, looking at that Cross, have changed their lives and committed themselves to living as authentic Christians. (...)

Nourished by the Eucharist, united to the Church and accepting your own crosses, ignite your own store of faith in the world! Proclaim divine mercy to everyone! Do not be afraid on this journey to entrust yourselves to Christ. You love the world of course, and that is good, because the world was made for human beings. However, at a certain point in life, it is necessary to make a radical choice. Without denying anything that is an expression of God's beauty or of the talents received from him, we must be able to side with Christ to witness before all to God's love. (...)

How different today's young people are from those of 20 years ago! How different is the cultural and social context in which we live! But Christ, no, he has not changed! He is the Redeemer of man yesterday, today and for ever! Put your talents, therefore, at the service of the new evangelization, to weave a new fabric of Christian life! The Pope is with you! Believe in Jesus, contemplate his Face, the Face of the crucified and risen Lord! That Face which so many long to see, but which is often veiled by our lack of enthusiasm for the Gospel and by our sin!

O beloved Jesus, reveal to us your Face of light and forgiveness! Look at us, renew us, send us out! Too many young people are waiting for you and if they do not see you they will not be able to live their vocation, they will not be able to live life for you and with you, to renew the world beneath your gaze which is turned to the Father and at the same time to our poor humanity.

Dear friends, with ever new creativity inspired by the Holy Spirit in prayer, continue together to carry the Cross that I entrusted to you 20 years ago. The young people of that time have changed just as I have, but your hearts, like mine, go on thirsting for truth, happiness, eternal life, and so they are ever young! This evening I put my trust in you once again, hope of the Church and of society! Do not be afraid! Take the power of the Cross everywhere, in season and out of season (CFR. 2 TM 4:2), so that everyone, also thanks to you, may continue to see and believe in the Redeemer of man!

Joannes Paulus II

1 April 2004, Address to the Roman youth at St Peter's Square

Prayer
to Blessed Pope John Paul II

God, our Father,
we want to extend to you our gratitude,
because You have given
to Your Holy Church
Blessed Pope John Paul II.
Through his dedication to Your divine mercy
and his love for the Virgin Mary,
through the power of the Holy Spirit,
he has become a shining example of
Jesus, the Good Shepherd.

We pray for Your Church:
- To remain faithful to the Gospel
- For purification and new prosperity
- Many vocations
- Blessing for the New Evangelisation
- And a deep love for Your Church.

Give to us by his intercession, and according to
Your will, the grace which we implore:
(insert your intention here)

Our Father...
Hail Mary...
Glory be...
Blessed Pope John Paul II, pray for us.